Revisiting Fatima

Susan M. Hogan, M.H.

REVISITING FATIMA

AS REVEALED BY THE GIFT OF A PHOTOGRAPH

BY SUSAN M. HOGAN, M. H.

Copyright Susan M. Hogan, November 8, 2016

This book is dedicated to the children of the world and preserving the Earth's resources for their future. The sale profits will help to fund The Genesis Project.

This publication was written for informational purposes only. The Food and Drug Administration (FDA) and U.S. Environmental Protection Agency (USEPA) have not evaluated these statements. The information is not intended to diagnose or treat disease. Always seek the advice of a licensed physician before changing medications or seeking treatment.

INTRODUCTION AND BOOK OVERVIEW

Revisiting the 1917 Fatima Apparitions brings to light an amazing series of unexplainable events and revelations revolving around the miracles that occurred and an extraordinary photograph taken in Fatima, Portugal. A copy of the photograph is on the cover of this book.

What happened in Fatima is very important to be aware of since over 50,000 witnesses saw the sun literally dance in the sky on October 13, 1917. Before the amazing miracle, Jesus' mother Mary appeared several times to three children from Fatima and relayed information concerning World Wars and other warnings. Even though the apparitions appeared 100 years ago, the messages carry great significance for what is happening today.

The continued importance of the apparitions has been reemphasized by mysterious, simultaneous changes to the Fatima photograph copies. Chapters 1 and 2 of this book include an account of the acquisition of the photograph and a summary of the distribution including the unexplainable activity witnessed by many people.

One famous person who received a copy of the photograph was Donald Trump. It was sent in a Bible quoting U.S. leaders who followed God before President Obama was elected. Why was Mr. Trump selected to receive this information before he ran for president? Was he predestined to become president and realize the importance of God's calling and guidance to lead? Could this intervention have occurred to reemphasize the importance of the 1917 Fatima Apparition on the timely 100-Year Anniversary?

During the 1917 Fatima Apparitions, Jesus' Mother held rosary beads and instructed the three children to pray the rosary every day. Mrs. Melania Trump held her precious rosary beads rather than a flower bouquet at their wedding. The Fatima photograph clearly depicts a figure holding prayer beads. While this unexplainable activity may seem hard to grasp, claims of divine intervention have been vindicated over time.

If you would like personal validation of the changing photograph mystery, you are encouraged to periodically monitor the photograph copy on the cover.

Chapter 3 delves deeper into the challenges humanity has faced relating to the timing and messages received during the Fatima Apparitions. Many subtle links are presented concerning historical mental, physical, and spiritual health. While researching the

Fatima Apparition and photograph changes, I found recurring themes concerning the environment's impact on health, especially of many famous religious figures.

The apparition timing and messages point to the importance of: protection of the sanctity of life; reinforcing basic moral values that are essential for developing and fortifying loving relationships; awareness that there is life after death; and the consequences of rejecting God. During one apparition, the children were shown hell and thereafter prayed constantly for souls to be saved from that fate.

Within three years of the apparitions, over 50 million people died from the Spanish Flu and World War I, the highest mortality statistic ever recorded. As a result of World War II 50 to 80 million people died. What was occurring at that time was a misuse of power and greed that has evolved and fed an insatiable appetite for causing harm without regard for humanity and love. The importance of the strong warning regarding World Wars became clearly event, since over time, fear, and a lasting lack of positive, open communication, have resulted in a global obsession to develop weapons of mass destruction. In 1917, Vladimir Lenin prepared the revolution in Russia that would overturn the Russian Social Order, which impacted the lives of a significant percentage of the world's population. During the apparitions, praying for Russia's conversion was specifically mentioned, and the end to World War I was predicted.

In 1920 the Russian Soviet Republic became the first country in the world to allow abortion in all circumstances. In 1916 Planned Parenthood was founded. Since 1980, almost a billion and a half abortions were performed worldwide according to the US Abortion Clock (usabortionclock.org) and the numbers are still ticking up.

Also apparent in the historical reflection upon the apparitions is the significance of the unprecedented threat to sustain health and life due to the pollution of the Earth's air, food, and water from the abuse of synthetic chemicals and radiation, many of which stemmed from the culture of war. The impact of these substances on life are linked to the apparitions' timing and warnings, especially relating to the existence of hell.

One startling recurring issue is the evolving danger from ingesting synthetic substances, which can result in the side effect of "suicide." Over time, what has become "acceptable or normal" has been perverted, making it important to educate oneself concerning the safety and use of a variety of manmade products.

There were several messages that were relayed by Jesus' Mother and one is referred to as "The Third Secret." There has been some controversy concerning the Vatican's revealing the true secret. This secret involved the possibility of future physical harm to a Pope and religious followers.

The warnings in the apparitions may at first seem to be negative; however, a loving mother would want her children to be close to her and avoid harm. The existence of a "bigger plan" through the Fatima Apparitions and the series of related remarkably interwoven events are brought to light to provide a path of hope that nothing is impossible with God. The apparitions were given as a gift to bring about global change, and help us to embrace the existence of a loving Father and the importance of the teachings and example of the Blessed Mother's Son, Jesus Christ. To love God above all, and in doing so, we will love one another and ourselves.

Our loving Father wisely created in a perfect way the resources we need to live happy and healthy lives. By honoring that wisdom, we can thrive and enjoy life. To assist you to have knowledge of the value of naturally occurring resources, chapter 4 includes samples of simple, low cost, abundant, and proven solutions. It seems ironic that what is often labeled "new age" or "alternative" was in fact the historical medicine replaced by modern science and technology.

The Closing Summary in chapter 5 provides a recap of the book's salient points and offers recommendations for reflections for adapting personally to the present state of humanity for preservation of mutual harmony and eternal peace, which is the message of the apparitions.

Anyone can present the past or list problems. It is the presence of Grace through that which is beyond comprehension and the existence of the divine that offers the perfect solutions based upon the collective knowledge and actions of perfect love, which are lavishly given to us as gifts.

While it is impossible to attempt to begin to fathom Grace, we can only try to do our best to share the gifts that have been given in an attempt to carry out what we are uniquely and individually called to accomplish. May this message bring rays of hope and love.

CHAPTER 1:
MARIAN APPARITIONS/THE PHOTOGRAPH

A. Marian Apparitions

A significant aspect of the Fatima events involved apparitions, specifically Marian Apparitions, which are an appearance or visitation by The Blessed Virgin Mary. Marian Apparitions are often named for the town where they occurred. While there have been many reports of apparitions and other contact with The Blessed Virgin Mary throughout history, some of the best known and well documented are Our Lady of Guadalupe, Our Lady of Lourdes, and Our Lady of Fatima. These apparitions occurred many years ago. Closer to our time, there have been reports of Marian Apparitions connected to Medjugorje, Bosnia and Herzegovina.

B. Miracle of Fatima

Several Marian apparitions involved the miraculous appearance of The Blessed Virgin Mary to a particular person, or small number of people. However, there are exceptions and one of these is Fatima.

The Fatima Apparition was witnessed by so many people, which validates that something very powerful and extraordinary occurred. One very important aspect of the October 13, 1917 apparition also involved Jesus being seen as a young child. Many Christians are awaiting the return of Jesus to Earth.

Some people tend to dismiss the idea of Marian Apparitions like Fatima for a variety of reasons, but the 1917 event was not limited to the apparition of The Blessed Virgin Mary. She did, however, play a prominent role in Fatima prior to that day, by teaching three children—Lucia, Jacinta, and Francisco—the importance of repentance, living a holy life based upon what her Son, Jesus Christ taught, and about life after death. The children also claimed to have been shown hell.

Death is not something most people like to dwell on, except when there is the hope for eternal life. The Fatima messages, like any other event considered unexplainable or a "miracle," are given only to make the world a better place and to help us grow in faith. This places our mortality into the correct perspective and assists others to act in a manner that is cognizant of the ramifications for inappropriate behavior and its impact on the world and others. When this "awareness" is not present, chaos can occur.

C. The Photograph

The amazing photograph on the cover was taken in Fatima, Portugal over twenty years ago. It was given to me to share with the world by a humble woman. In this book, she will be referred to as "Elizabeth."

A series of events leading up to the acquisition of the photograph copy and subsequent observations are provided for your review and reflection.

Even if you are not Catholic or are uncertain about the existence of God, I encourage you to research the event that thousands of people witnessed in Fatima.

As you continue to read, you will be amazed at the links to the past that are being witnessed today.

1. Elizabeth's Story

I first encountered Elizabeth when she visited a retail store I developed in 2002. The store had all forms of herbal formulas and botanical products. She was seeking assistance for her husband who had been diagnosed with cancer. Evidently, other employees he closely worked with were also diagnosed with cancer. She said they had been exposed to a lot of chemicals during their employment at a local military base.

Elizabeth told me her husband had been to an oncologist who gave him a prognosis of about three months to live. The couple refused to resign him to such a short life span. They found a different oncologist, one who was more positive and was also receptive to using natural formulas in addition to modern Western Medicine.

We discussed the situation, and Elizabeth decided to purchase an herbal formula of maitake mushroom in the hope that it would assist her husband as he progressed through chemotherapy. A product to naturally increase his blood PH was also purchased.

She returned a few times to buy more of the products since the oncologist felt they were helping. It was a long time before I saw her again.

2. The Acquisition of the Photograph

Several years after our last encounter, I telephoned a local business to inquire about a bill. To my surprise, the person that answered the call was Elizabeth. She told me her husband was doing well and mentioned the great progress he recently made with a UMAC Phytoplankton supplement he had been taking that amazed his doctor. His blood work was in range after six months.

She mentioned a very serious injustice with her husband's medical claims that she had just found out about earlier that day. Evidently, the medication her husband had been taking for several years was available for thousands of dollars less per dose than what they were being charged. She was prompted to investigate the situation after speaking with a pharmaceutical representative who was surprised with the hospital's significant mark up.

Elizabeth said she questioned the cost variance with the hospital and they said it was because the drug required refrigeration. Cost variations between hospitals, especially for chemical therapy, can differ substantially. I offered to help them since I have experience in health benefit consulting. Elizabeth had been previously unaware of my consulting background.

I visited her several times to discuss the billing situation. During one discussion, she mentioned a very strange event in which her husband was prayed over by a preacher after having been diagnosed with cancer. She said the CAT scan was clear thereafter, but the cancer came back. (Perhaps because he continued to be exposed to the toxic chemicals at his work?)

While attempting to help Elizabeth with the claims, we talked about prayer, and I commented on how The Blessed Virgin Mary's prayers, and reciting the rosary, had helped me in so many aspects of my life. She then told me she was Catholic when she was younger and mentioned the photograph of the lady holding the beads at Fatima she had in her bedroom.

This is what Elizabeth said about the picture: "Many years ago I gave a disposable camera to a friend of mine who was planning a trip to Fatima. I asked her to take a picture of the oak holm tree where an apparition occurred. When my friend returned, she telephoned and said she felt it to be a holy place, but she and her companions did not see anything unusual." Elizabeth then gave her friend permission to look at the developed photographs taken with the disposable camera. Elizabeth's friend was so surprised at what she saw, she screamed over the telephone. At the oak holm tree she had photographed, another image was visible. "The negative for the picture did not have the mysterious image in it, the figure could only be seen on the printed picture."

The mysterious image was of a woman holding strands of beads. Evidently, Elizabeth kept the original photograph in her bedroom in a simple frame for about twenty years. She gave it to me to copy for an elder in our parish who had shared his experiences at Marian Apparition sites with the religious education class I taught. When I received the photograph the main female figure holding the beads and the tree were the only visible images other than the sky and ground.

CHAPTER 2:
UNEXPLAINABLE EVENTS RELATING TO
THE PHOTOGRAPH COPIES

A. The Photograph Copies Begin to Change

A fascinating aspect of the photograph are the changes that have been occurring in copies made without known human intervention. Three days after I had taken the original to a local store to be enlarged and copied, I noticed two darker areas that appeared like eyes next to the main figure, one above each shoulder. Elizabeth and her husband also began noticing changes in their enlarged copy, although we were both initially reluctant to talk about what was happening.

I then began handing out photograph copies to friends, including people from the church I attend, who also witnessed unexplainable changes in their copies.

Cardinal Timothy Dolan was sent the photograph a few weeks after I attended a Mass at St. Patrick's Cathedral in New York City. During Mass, he emphasized the importance of respecting life, especially of the unborn. Two crossed staffs mysteriously appeared in the photograph copies shortly after it was sent. The new images reminded people of the keys on the Pope's Coat of Arms. The Cardinal has received the photograph copy several times in other correspondence and graciously responded in writing to the ideas presented. However, he did not acknowledge the changing photograph.

Several months later, I felt prompted to send a copy of the photograph to Donald Trump. Over eight years ago his name came across my mind rather strongly after Communion and before I received the Chalice when I attended a local Daily Mass. I knew very little about Mr. Trump. This happened again unexpectedly several years later.

I sent Mr. Trump the photograph in a Bible about U.S. politicians' before the election of President Obama. Several years later, while praying at night with my eyes closed, I saw a glimpse of people dancing and a large diamond ring. A few days after, I read a news story about the Trumps' recent anniversary where they were dancing with Mrs. Trump's rosary beads. The news story indicated that she held rosary beads rather than a bridal bouquet when they were married. She grew up close to Medjugorje where apparitions are reported to occur frequently.

I have sent Mr. Trump correspondence several times over the past eight years, hoping he would realize the significance of the Grace involved. I have never received any acknowledgment of the correspondence. Over the last eight years, I have relayed what occurred regarding Mr. Trump, the photograph, the Bible, and the vision to several people. I was often alienated at the mention of what transpired at the Chalice. After he was elected president, people have responded in a very positive manner to my previous comments regarding Mr. Trump's importance. The abortion issue may have tipped the election in his favor.

B. Padre Pio's Appearance in the Photograph

Over time, people have commented on other images seen in the photograph. Several people saw St. Padre Pio's image. St. Padre Pio is the Roman Catholic Patron Saint of the Unborn who worked to develop a model concept of a hospital in Italy. Many miracles occurred during his lifetime including the stigmata, which are representative of the wounds of Christ. He had a special devotion to the rosary and The Blessed Virgin Mary, who was reported to appear to him. He also suffered for most of his life from a mysterious lung condition.

C. The Photograph is Sent to The Vatican

In December of 2012, a shadow of a woman's face appeared next to the face of the main image. The shadow face appeared very sad.

Shortly thereafter, a friend called me and said the main image in his photograph copy appeared to be crying. He urged me to send a copy of the photograph to Pope Benedict XVI.

Someone commented on the appearance of an image of what looked like a fetus in the photo left of the main image's head after sending the photocopy to the Vatican.

Perhaps this relates to the sale of unborn baby tissue and increased prevalence of abortions? The use of fetal cells and condoned killing of innocent babies for medical purposes is viewed by many as an acceptable practice. The need to use human cells for science is interesting to ponder as it relates to Jesus' teaching and the concept of Padre Pio's model hospital and designation as the Patron Saint of the Unborn. Planned Parenthood was founded in 1916 right before the apparitions.

As you read through this book, it will become even more apparent how the subject of health and protection of life in all forms was interwoven into the Fatima messages.

There have been several U.S. hospitals in which modern Marian apparitions have been reported to be witnessed. Perhaps there is a connection?

D. The Unexplainable Image on the Refrigerator

One parishioner of our local church said an image of the figure with the beads remained on the refrigerator door after the photograph copy was removed for cleaning. Her family witnessed it and they tried to come up with a logical reason for the presence of the image, but could not.

Could the incident have occurred on a refrigerator to reflect the need for change in how our food is grown and processed and our modern diets?

Heavy reliance on synthetic substances that cause harm has led to pollution of air, food and water that support life. In many parts of the world, the importation of genetically engineered plant matter and many agricultural chemicals have been prohibited. Certainly, there must be solid scientific rationale for the banning of these substances.

Inhumane treatment of animals, injection of antibiotics and hormones, and increased use of toxic pesticides and incomplete forms of fertilizers is rampant among large, commercialized farmers in many parts of the world. The impact to health and plant regrowth over time is unknown. Certain nutritional deficiencies may already be posing common threats to health.

For example, when organic phosphorous is deficient in food that is consumed, human ailments such as arthritis, formation of stones, and inability to fully utilize other minerals can occur.

Another problem, stemming from World War II, was the excessive use of nitrogen in fertilizers that was left over from manufacturing weapons. Excessive synthesized nitrogen can result in algae blooms or depletion of organic soils.

It seems only logical that the use of synthetic substances would create an imbalance in nature. Why would farmers use a substance that blows up to grow plants and why would anyone knowingly eat that food?

The side effects of synthetic pesticides that often target the pest's neurological system are well documented, especially on developing young children. Their body size and lack of protection offered through immature blood brain barrier development could be related to the increases in autism, attention deficit disorder, and poor neurological health.

Deviation from what was created to nutritionally support health has resulted in unprecedented obesity, with accumulation of toxins, which can increase the risk of cancer, heart disease, and diabetes. Fertility and the ability to reproduce may also be impacted.

After all of the time and money invested in modern medical research, there is no "cure" for these common diseases. There is, however, consensus that exercise, whole food organic diets, stress management, and prayer may help prevent and cure disease.

The primary way to reduce the toxic load and excessive consumption is through discipline and avoidance. The importance of fasting or abstaining has been recorded many times during Biblical history as well as during many Marian Apparitions. Perhaps these practices are recommended for our own good, to strengthen us, help us to think clearly, and bring us back to the way we were originally created so we could enjoy a closer relationship with one another and God.

E. Changes After the Epiphany and Frankincense

In January of 2014, a day after the Epiphany is celebrated, someone noticed images that appeared in gold on the middle bottom of the photograph. They looked like a person riding an animal following a star with a pack animal trailing. This seemed rather timely for the celebration of the Magis' visit to Jesus.

One of the gifts the Magi brought was frankincense. Frankincense has long been used in religious ceremonies. Frankincense has also been researched extensively for its medicinal value.

There has been quite a bit of research concerning frankincense and cancer, including pancreatic cancer, breast cancer, and so on. If you are interested in reviewing information concerning the published clinical studies, they can be found by searching under Pub Med, frankincense (Boswellia), and cancer.

Frankincense has also been researched for its positive impact on the brain and pineal gland, the mysterious gland in the head. In addition to its benefits for cancer, there have been clinical studies for its value to repair DNA. Frankincense is a very important resource for our modern world.

Won't helping people to regain the ability to think and pray in closer unity with God be an important priority for miracles to occur?

F. Reports of Visions of the Image in the Photograph

One day while I was sitting at Eucharistic Adoration at church, praying for guidance, a woman came into the church crying. She was in a lot of pain and had been having trouble with her medical treatment and bills. I gave her a copy of the photograph and an essential oil and we prayed together for her healing.

A few days later she told me she saw the same image of the lady in the photograph holding the beads in the night sky. She was diagnosed many months later with another serious health issue that required multiple hospitalizations and surgical procedures. She has experienced lasting complications as a result of her surgical treatment.

There have been two other people who have told me they saw a vision of the main image a day before they saw the photograph. It seemed odd that the three people who saw the visions were dealing with severe, recurring digestive health ailments. They have suffered from complications and were burdened with the costs of their medical treatment.

Since the digestive tract is also involved with immunity and the production of hormones, the side effects of some modified foods or synthetic chemicals may cause mental disorders, including suicide. This is certainly a concern if one were to contemplate the existence of hell and warnings during the Fatima Apparitions.

Therefore, the impact of synthetic chemicals on physical health and mental well being should be an important consideration for leaders of religious organizations.

G. The Native American Image

Several years ago, a friend told me he noticed a change in the photograph that appeared to be a Native American chieftain. The image was where the left arm of the main figure had been. Since he received the photograph, he watches it frequently and has noted many changes.

Native Americans had great respect for the sanctity of nature, the divine, and relied upon their ancestor's knowledge and use of plants and animals for healing.

The ability to protect vast amounts of land they considered to be precious was taken away from them.

Another call perhaps to respect and protect the rights of people and the environment?

H. The Sick Horse and the Changes in the Photograph

While praying the rosary one day, I received a thought about a horse. The next day a woman I had helped many years ago who experienced an unexplainable healing event telephoned me and said she received a message from God instructing her to call me. Her horse was sick with a fungus infection in its eye. The horse was taken to an animal hospital, but she was concerned about the other horses she owned. She rescues abused animals.

This was rather curious, since I had previously been intimidated by the size and strength of horses, and have never received training in animal medicine. I knew I could not ignore the request, so I went to the woman's barn. We prayed together and she applied essential plant oils I blended. The barn was also diffused with the oils. The horses responded positively.

The day after I met with her and the horses, I saw horses in the photograph, especially in the upper left hand side, and other people reported seeing horses in it.

A few months later, the horse that was diagnosed with the eye infection and sent to the animal hospital was returned to her. The medical care had become very expensive and the horse's behavior was difficult to manage. Recovery was then aided by a change in diet and the periodic application of essential oils.

There seemed to be a correlation between the horse, Elizabeth, and the medicines.

The horse's fungus medicine also had to be refrigerated.

During the course of my health claim consulting work, I have noted that many medicines have been recalled due to the presence of mold or fungus. Modern medical practitioners seem to have a limited amount of success when dealing with fungus, molds, and mildew. The side effects of fungal drugs provide strong cautions for necessity of use. Many other types of medicines carry warnings concerning lowered immunity to fungus, and contain warnings if the patient resides in a particular geographic area.

If medications require refrigeration for preservation, what happens when they are injected into a warm blooded mammal? Why are they so expensive? Could there be long term complications for their use similar to antibiotics that result in the growth of unwanted pathogens such as candida and H pylori due to die-off of beneficial pathogen protection? The importance of preserving and increasing the strength of the complex cells in our digestive tract for health is gaining great attention in clinical studies.

The modern, standardized approach of using substances like antibiotics, antibacterials, antifungals, and so on that "kill" appears to be causing a wide set of problems such as resistant infections and all sorts of mutations. Beneficial pathogens in every aspect of our environment are very important for sustaining health and life through balance.

Most botanicals are selective, which means they destroy harmful pathogens while protecting those that benefit. Isn't the use of plants and natural resources more in line with what we have been historically taught? The Bible references plants as "good" from the beginning of creation. Throughout history respected and knowledgeable figures such as Hippocrates and Muhammad cited plants as important for humankind. Could this be another warning to us for needed change to protect our Earth and life?

I. The Face in the Beads

In December of 2013, a feminine face blowing a kiss appeared in one of the beads to the right of the middle of the main image. Next to it, an image of a dog's head also appeared. This, and many other faces, were discovered after the photograph was reviewed by magnification.

J. The Miracle Healing and Miraculous Medal

Unexplainable healing through prayer has also been a recurring theme surrounding the photograph. As an example, someone commented on seeing the Miraculous Medal appear in the right upper corner of the photograph around the time her friend was unexplainably cured of terminal cancer. She had been praying the rosary for his recovery while holding the Miraculous Medal in her hand in front of the photograph.

The Miraculous Medal symbol was a gift given during a Marian Apparition that occurred in 1806 in Paris, France. St. Catherine Labouré was instructed by The Blessed Virgin Mary to have two images struck on a medal that was to be distributed and worn to receive special graces. The front of the medal depicts The Blessed Virgin Mary standing on a globe, with the head of a serpent beneath her feet. Circling the oval-shaped medal is the signature, "O Mary, conceived without sin, pray for us who have recourse to thee." On the reverse, twelve stars surround a large "M," from which a cross arises. Below the "M," the medal depicts two flaming hearts. The left heart, circled with thorns, represents Jesus. The right heart, pierced by a sword, symbolizes Mary.

The first image on the medal is consistent with the Our Lady of Guadalupe image that miraculously appeared on an article of clothing worn by Juan Diego who reported seeing a vision of The Blessed Virgin Mary in Guadalupe. Our Lady of Guadalupe is another well-known Catholic Church–approved Marian Apparition.

It was rather shocking to learn that not long after the unexplainable healing from cancer occurred, the friend that was prayed for died in an accident. His unexplainable recovery certainly must have had an impact on his faith, as well as the faith of those who knew him.

Spontaneous, unexplainable healing after prayer certainly can provide confirmation of the existence of the divine, boosting faith. This supports a main consideration of the Fatima Apparition, to help save souls.

The guidance of souls to heaven is interesting to ponder. During Christ's life on Earth he was aware of the existence of spirits. His presence helped those who were suffering from unclean spirits and miracles of healing occurred. A diversity of cultures also believe in the existence of spirits who can influence behavior. If an unclean spirit were present at the time of death, could it be possible that the welfare of the soul might be affected?

Are the apparitions being given to us as a gift that can help us develop close, loving spiritual relationships that would protect us from evil spirits on Earth and thereafter? During apparitions including Fatima, The Blessed Mother provided reassurance that she would help souls at the time of death.

K. Historical Importance of Prayer with Beads/Significance of Fatima

As you will note, the main image in the photograph is holding a large strand of beads. A smaller set of beads similar to the rosary can be faintly seen around the neck.

One can only speculate, but the large set of beads could possibly be symbolic of the old tradition of reciting the 150 Psalms. In addition, the historical use of prayer beads in many ancient religions throughout the world is noteworthy. Is this a sign for the need for loving prayer in the world?

A Muslim Princess is linked to the Fatima name. Fatima was the daughter of Muhammad who converted to Christianity during the time of the Reconquista, a turbulent period of violence. The name of Fatima is associated with peace.

Could the promotion of peace and unity in such a divided world today have been another reason for the selection of Fatima as the sight for the apparition witnessed by thousands?

L. Summary of the Changes and Final Distribution Efforts

As time went on, more and more images have appeared in the photograph copies. There have been too many changes to list. Whether the copy is on electronic media or paper doesn't seem to matter. When the copies are enlarged on a computer or telephone, many images and faces are in it. Some of the larger original copies seem to be fading.

Several years ago, the photograph was placed in two books I wrote in an effort to help people view the photograph changes personally. Since the photograph seemed to involve modern issues, and the Fatima predictions, the books were written with the objective of helping people to understand the significance of the changes that have been occurring in the environment with an emphasis on health, including the value of botanicals; basic moral principles; and the history of humankind based on Biblical stories, especially the inception, birth, life, death, and resurrection of Jesus. The specific Biblical names were omitted to enable the books to be shared in public places.

When the Ukraine was invaded by Russia several years ago, people commented that the main image's face on the photograph, which had been feminine, began to resemble male features—especially a dark area resembling facial hair. The timing was of concern, because the changes appeared to relate to the 1917 Fatima Apparition warnings relating to Russia's Errors that involve what is referred to as the Third Secret of Fatima. There has been controversy concerning whether the Vatican has accurately released the secret to the world. Whether the Vatican has fulfilled the request made during the apparition by The Blessed Mother for consecration of Russia to her heart is another concern prayed for by many who have interest in Marian Apparitions.

Due to the photograph changes and timing after the Ukraine was attacked, I decided to send the photograph to the Bishop's Office in the Catholic Diocese in Raleigh, North Carolina. Their response stated that to pursue the apparition approval by the Catholic Church required the Diocese where the event took place reviewing the information. I then sent a copy of the photograph to the Roman Catholic Diocese in Fatima. No response was received.

A few days before the November 2015 Paris terrorist attack, a friend and I both witnessed a change in the photograph copy's main image's face. We both felt it clearly looked like Jesus. The photograph copy we were looking at was posted on the wall of a priest's house. We were discussing world affairs.

The activity in the Middle East, Russia's intervention, the history of Fatima, and the warnings are no coincidence and demonstrate the need for us to pay attention to what is happening and to pray for world peace and unity. During the time of the nuclear talks with Iran, I was contacted by someone who noted what appeared to be two radiation symbols in the photograph.

What is happening globally with thousands of people having to flee from their homeland may be significant for the Fatima event. One of the children who witnessed the apparition wrote of a time when the Pope would be extremely upset since he was surrounded by masses of hungry people.

A large influx of grown immigrants that do not have the ability to communicate in a native language and who follow different cultural beliefs, especially the rejection of the role of a woman who may be assigned to assist them, is problematic for all concerned. Italy has been reported to have thousands of immigrants who are being jailed.

The selection for the location of the Fatima Apparition, the third secret, the 100th anniversary and its relationship with Muslim history, are interesting to ponder. World leaders' reaction to acceptance of people from Muslim countries and immigrants seems rather timely too. Wouldn't it be wonderful if there was a globally coordinated effort to help people suffering this great tragedy to live freely in peace and abundance in places that are not occupied?

It may seem hard to believe that these events took place; therefore, the presence of the photograph copy on the cover is provided for your observation. If you look carefully at the photograph, you will be amazed to see many images that are masterfully woven together. Over time, check the photograph for unexplainable changes, and ask yourself, "How can that happen?"

CHAPTER 3:
HEALTH, DEATH, AND DISEASES IN RELATION TO THE FATIMA APPARITIONS AND WARNINGS

A. Fatima Apparitions and Warnings/The Practices Recommended

It was reported that over 50 million people died (a mortality statistic of the highest historical significance recorded on Earth), due to the Spanish Flu and war from the time of the 1917 apparition through 1920.

As mentioned previously, the children at Fatima claimed to witness hell before this record number of deaths began to occur. In addition to the predictions that were given to the children at Fatima, which came true, warnings concerning possible future worldly events, including the annihilation of countries, were also provided.

During the October 13, 1917 event in Fatima, which was witnessed by over 50,000 people, spinning and strange activity of the sun was seen. These unexplainable, profound changes brought heightened attention to those who witnessed the event. Many were in fear of their lives, and thought it was the end of the world. In addition to The Blessed Virgin Mary's appearance, Jesus as a child and St. Joseph were also reported to be seen by witnesses.

The weather during the apparition included a dark sky with rain. Thereafter, the sun came out and everything became dry. The sun appeared to move toward the Earth, zig zagging.

While many of the 1917 Fatima Apparition warnings and predictions have been publicly revealed and appropriately been officially interpreted to relate to eternal salvation through the importance of loving God and one another, other factors unfolded.

It is notable that extreme solar activity has been studied for the impact on the Earth's weather, although conclusive evidence may be lacking. Perhaps this somehow relates to the message given at Fatima with the radical weather changes we are experiencing and the strange weather activity during the apparition?

Solar flares can halt access to electricity, which we have become so dependent on. If the flares were severe, the activity could significantly affect how we conduct our lives.

Humankind's abuse of natural resources and the manipulation of nature through machines is also something to contemplate. Severe adverse weather events lead to increased profitability for many corporations. Could the Fatima miracle have been a warning to us to protect the environment and use technology only for the good of life on Earth?

Another timely event involves Russia. The children who were present at the Fatima Apparitions said that The Blessed Virgin Mary told them that God wanted consecration to her Immaculate Heart for salvation—especially for prayer for the Consecration of Russia.

The thought of people placing such importance upon The Blessed Virgin Mary's consecration may seem inappropriate to many, but God did choose The Blessed Virgin Mary to conceive Jesus through The Holy Spirit. Her Son's presence on Earth was meant to save us. The events of her life provided a bridge between humanity and the divine.

During her lifetime, Jesus' Mother lovingly responded to God's will with humility and obedience. She was the only human present at the conception of Jesus. What other human could have shared accurate details with the Apostles who wrote the New Testament concerning Jesus' conception and early life than his Mother?

The Blessed Mother insisted that her Son share his miracle at the wedding at Cana.

When her Son was crucified, she was one of the few followers present. She endured a Mother's terrible suffering, yet forgave her Son's persecutors, while trusting totally in God.

The events of her life with Jesus are what is contemplated as the rosary is recited. Perhaps that is why the children at Fatima were given instructions from The Blessed Virgin Mary to recite the rosary daily. She also encouraged attendance at frequent confession with true repentance for sin. Having one profess their mistakes openly and deeply, believing in receiving total forgiveness, is a wonderful thing.

The importance of receiving Holy Communion (Eucharist) has also been a frequent message at Marian Apparitions. Miracles have been reported in connection with the Eucharist, such as laboratory analysis of the composition to be from a living human. These were cited as important practices that would assist souls to receive protection, especially during the time of tribulation, and to go to heaven.

It was reported that The Blessed Virgin Mary was also holding the brown scapular during the apparition. The brown scapular is a religious item that is well known for providing protection. True life stories of protection concerning the brown scapular and the rosary are interesting to research. In one story, priests reciting the rosary near where the atom bomb was dropped were reported to be protected from the event.

The importance of reciting the rosary daily has been emphasized during many apparitions. The rosary is often misunderstood as being a Catholic prayer. It actually involves praying to the Holy Spirit of God, praying The Our Father, while reciting Hail Mary's during the contemplation of Jesus' life based upon The Blessed Virgin Mary's personal witness and awareness of what occurred.

The Hail Mary is asking Jesus' Mother to pray for us. It is a common, and loving gesture for people to request prayers from one another, or to pray for those who have died. Why not lovingly ask someone who had such a close relationship with Jesus and God to pray for us? Why wouldn't that be a wise or acceptable thing to do?

During the Fatima Apparitions, the children were also told to say a prayer asking Jesus for mercy, to forgive sins and lead souls to heaven. This was to be prayed while reciting the rosary.

The three children from Fatima frequently offered up personal sacrifice, such as giving their meal to the poor, for the salvation of souls. They were very concerned about the souls they saw in hell.

B. The Fatima Events, Religious Figures and Respiratory Conditions

While many of the 1917 Fatima Apparition warnings and predictions have been publicly revealed and officially interpreted to relate to significant and important issues including World Wars I and II, a new twist to the message began to unfold as unusual events occurred. The strange weather activity at Fatima seemed to be connected.

A few years ago, while looking for some items for my house in a thrift store, I was clearly and unexpectedly led in thought to the book sale area where I found a small book that was hidden between two other books sitting on a bottom shelf. It was called *Princesses of the Kingdom*, written by Leo Madigan who has since passed away, although the importance of his work is being perpetuated.

Leo Madigan's book told the story of Jacinta Marta who was one of the children at Fatima, and Nellie Organ, another child who claimed to witness miracles involving Jesus.

After I left the thrift shop, I realized I was very near the church where I was scheduled to volunteer to be present at Eucharist Adoration. I remembered my obligation because the Monstrous, which holds the Communion Host during Adoration, was pictured on the cover of the little book.

While driving to church, I thought about how peaceful it would be to sit at Adoration and not have to deal with the thought of other people's health problems and the monetary costs that were so excessive and burdensome, with often failed results.

I knelt down and prayed, then felt it was important to read the little book. I read about Jacinta who suffered and died at a very young age. The child, Nellie, also died young. So did most of her family. The book mentioned little Nellie living in a cold, damp place.

It was surprising to read about Jacinta suffering from ill health, including consumption (tuberculosis, "TB"), and evidently, her parents could no longer afford medical treatment at a hospital and were sent home. Jacinta died shortly after a surgical procedure while confined at a second hospital. Evidently, she had a large hole in her chest as a result of surgery. I realized then that the suffering that occurred in the little Fatima witnesses was part of a bigger plan that would be revealed to the world many years later.

Unlike Jacinta and Francisco who also witnessed the apparitions, the third child to witness the event, Lucia, did not die young, although she suffered from a respiratory disease later in life. The respiratory issues just kept coming up.

In the book *FATIMA in Lucia's Own Words*, Lucia indicated that The Blessed Mother had warned that Jacinta would be confined to two hospitals and would die alone in the second hospitalization, although the Blessed Mother also let Jacinta know that she would be present to help her to go to heaven.

Lucia's book seems to be the truest account of Fatima I have read. I strongly recommend it as a means of personally putting into perspective how morality has declined in our modern world. The humble account of the young children's witness, faith, suffering, courage, and love is very inspirational. The truth concerning the apparitions seemed unquestionable. There were also many subtle "coincidences" concerning the connection between health and spirituality that involved the children.

Over time, further patterns kept coming up that emphasized the relative significance of the adverse health the children and their families suffered. This included several Catholic saints who also had illnesses, especially respiratory conditions, around the time of the Fatima Apparitions. The Saints included Padre Pio who was seen in the Fatima photograph on the cover of this book by several people.

The link to health was heightened while watching a film called *Padre Pio between Heaven and Earth*. The movie depicted the Padre suffering severely from an undiagnosable respiratory condition after leaving an old monastery in his youth. I wondered if mold or mildew exposure was the cause? Later in the movie, he was coughing as he held the Communion during Mass.

He was also depicted in his elderly years as being severely ill, and coughing, immediately before a miraculous healing occurred. His health was restored while he was holding a rosary and watching a traveling statue of The Blessed Mother, created to remember the Fatima Apparition. The statue was being transported by helicopter from the hospital St. Padre Pio worked to build.

St. Padre Pio's model hospital in Italy focuses on restoring health in the mind, body, and spirit. St. Padre Pio realized the importance of healthy food for the hospital patients and he selected a chef to run the hospital's kitchen under his spiritual direction. The hospital owns two local farms. His hospital was to be a model for other Catholic hospitals. A section of the hospital is also dedicated to serving those who need spiritual cleansing and mortification. The Eucharist was reported to be present daily.

St. Francis Kolbe was another Saint that seemed to be connected to the Fatima message. After researching his life, I learned that he suffered from TB. Like St. Padre Pio, he was also considered to be a Patron Saint of the Unborn. He is also the Patron Saint of chemical dependency. St. Kolbe died in an Auschwitz death camp when he volunteered his life to save another prisoner who had a family.

Many priests were persecuted in the camps. Drugs like Pervitin, a type of methamphetamine, used heavily by soldiers during World War II, are connected to violent, bizarre behavior. Could the use of these drugs lift their consciences, enabling them to commit horrible acts toward innocent men, women, and children?

While methamphetamines differ from amphetamines which are so frequently prescribed and abused today, the imbalance of brain chemistry, including a decrease in dopamine that may lead to further addiction, can be an issue.

Amphetamine treatment for the young today is unprecedented. There is more than double the rate of boys who are diagnosed with attention deficit disorder than girls, and the published figures do not include self-prescribed abuse of prescriptions to enhance energy and performance on tests in our highly competitive world. Sudden, horrific violence like school shootings generally involve young males.

Could there be a connection with the long-term drug side effects and behavior that lacks conscience? If access to the drugs ceased, would the many offenders and their victims suffering finally be helped? Could this horrific behavior have been another reason for the Fatima warning for what was to come?

Over time, the re-emphasis on the need to provide physical, spiritual, and mental care, in addition to acute care, like at St. Padre Pio's hospital became apparent.

Another surprise was learning of St. Gemma Galgani who lived from 1878–1903. Her life served as an inspiration for both St. Francis Kolbe and St. Padre Pio. St. Gemma Galgani's Mother died of TB when she was only seven years old.

Later in life, the Saint was diagnosed with TB in her spine. She was treated with cautery and was placed in an iron corset. The recollection of her suffering from the medical treatment was reported by her family to be horrific. The medical care did not cure the young saint. Evidently, the medical cost caused her family significant financial hardship. Later in life, St. Galgani was reported to have had a miraculous healing through the visitation of the Archangel Raphael who encouraged her to recite the rosary.

The night I wrote about St. Gemma Galgani, I thought, "How many other religious people have died from respiratory diseases?" The next day, I attended Mass, and the priest announced the saint of the day was Saint Thérèse of Lisieux. She is the patron Saint of Lung Ailments and Missions. The priest said she died of TB at the age of 24. I had heard about Saint Thérèse, known as The Little Flower of Jesus, but never researched her health.

Evidently, St. Thérèse suffered another severe illness at a young age and saw a vision of The Blessed Virgin Mary smiling at her while praying in front of a statue of her. She was then miraculously healed.

St. Thérèse was reported to have lived in a cold convent when she later developed TB and died. During St. Thérèse's life, she was considered to be quite ordinary. She did not work in missions but was responsible for cleaning the convent. However, after her death, her writings were circulated and she became one of the most well-known saints.

It seemed appropriate to search the internet to determine what other religious figures died from TB. Another famous saint was St. Maria Faustina Kolwalska. This is the saint most well known for visitations by Jesus. The Divine Mercy Chaplet is a prayer associated with the visitations that requests mercy from God through the contemplation of Jesus Christ's passion and the image of rays of light pouring out from his heart. St. Faustina also had something in common with St. Thérèse; she was assigned simple tasks in the convent.

She was also living in the same town as St. Francis Kolbe during his religious life. While TB is a communicable disease, being weakened from living in an old, damp, cold building certainly would predispose one to ill health.

The lives of the saints, including the true story of the little children of Fatima, were so remarkable. In addition to the many miracles, there were so many elective sacrifices of purposely living in harsh conditions, without complaint, for the love of God and example to others.

Each life story had its own unique path, and a purpose in history. Sharing God's Earthly gifts to help humanity is a great service. Using the gifts that God provides on Earth for strength and vigor seems good and appropriate to enhance the ability to serve.

A few months prior to finding the *Princesses of the Kingdom* book, and learning about the saints' health, I had discovered an archived book written in 1914 regarding a natural and cheap cure for Consumption ("TB") that involved a substance referred to as "kerosene." Kerosene, when used and formulated correctly, possessed important medicinal value. It was not the kerosene we use today, which is toxic. Evidently, it was derived from either pine or from unrefined crude oil. The recipe for it was not provided in the book. Other archived information discussed in chapter 4 of this book involves the historical use of pine derivatives for restorative health, including TB.

C. Link between Fatima Events, Weather, and Air Quality

The historical relationship between adverse extreme weather events that result in flooding and plague-like diseases, such as the Spanish Flu, and the impact on indoor air and health are interesting to ponder. The Bible does mention mildew and blasts, and the Biblical timing of pestilence is noteworthy.

As far as indoor air quality is concerned, a logical pattern was present. Religious leaders, the poor and those who serve the poor, as well as children, would be at greater risk for respiratory conditions and weakened immunity from living in old buildings, missions, and schools. Homes of the elderly and old hospitals would also be prone to leaks and poor indoor air quality as well as lead, asbestos, and other environmental hazards.

The health of the thymus gland located in the chest area is very important for strong immunity. If it is compromised due to pathogens or toxins, the body will have difficulty maintaining health.

Modern scientists have now claimed to reconstruct the Spanish Flu (that killed millions after 1917) from old infected cadavers, in an attempt to learn more about the disease that severely impacted soldiers who were in the prime of their life. They determined that each cadaver also suffered from pneumonia. Could the old government buildings or indoor air quality have been a factor? Could the Spanish Flu have been man-made? Man-made chemical or biological weapon experimentation was also evolving at the time of the 1917 apparition.

The health issues caused by mold, mildew, and toxic indoor air pollution was a subject that seemed to keep coming up in my work, especially since the time the photograph was acquired.

It is interesting that pathogens, including bacteria like TB, thrive on wet environments. These pathogens can grow near the mold, and if breathed in can wreak havoc on health. In addition to the pathogens, the mold spores can absorb the material they grow on as well as other toxins that are present. Toxic chemicals in fabrics, paints, and so on, which are present in the furnishings or interiors, also adversely impact health.

If indoor environments are routinely sprayed for pests or pathogens, this presents another threat for toxin exposure. If toxic chemicals are used for cleaning, there could be severe issues if mold or mildew spores absorb the toxins and they are breathed in.

There were several incidences that were brought to my attention that involved serious health issues, including cancer, after renovations of schools and other buildings. To have three children who attended the same school, being diagnosed with the same rare cancer, around the same time was one of the unusual situations. There were others who suffered serious health issues after being in buildings that were sprayed or renovated.

In one charity I visited, there were frequent infestations of insects that were treated with pesticides. The workers at the charity were very ill after the treatment, and the cost strained their budget.

It was also noted that mold and mildew from leaking buildings frequently resulted in the need for biocides or harsh chemicals to be used in places where children spend large amounts of time indoors.

Discussions concerning this subject provided unexpected comments. Evidently, air conditioning was uncommon in many buildings in the south years ago, so old schools were purposefully built with flat roofs. The roofs would collect water to cool the buildings, but the windows were kept open in hot weather. A very simple solution was to open up the windows and doors.

Due to cost considerations, it became obvious that there was a greater chance for the improper use of chemicals that can be hazardous to health. In particular, the use of bleach is often not supervised, and may be ineffective in some cases. Many professional mold specialists do not consider bleach to be an effective biocide for all strains of mold and mildew. Some use essential oils such as thyme and orange in their biocides.

Synthetic chemicals are generally not selective and as a result may kill beneficial microorganisms that provide natural protection. Pathogens can mutate, being very difficult to destroy.

The high rate of statistics relative to the presence of mold in homes and schools is noteworthy but, of course, will fluctuate based on the area and weather history.

As noted from years of review of medical claims in my work, mold toxicity is not something many physicians typically diagnosis in patients; therefore, the use of medications may only cover up or worsen symptoms. Mold toxicity may also be linked to many diseases besides respiratory conditions, such as vascular disorders, psychiatric conditions, and one mold specialist even connected it to diabetes.

The impact of toxic modern indoor air quality could be having a very serious impact on the endocrine system, especially the thymus gland. Young children, the immune compromised, and elderly would be at greater health risk due to the problems with indoor air, especially during times of extreme weather variations when people spend a good percentage of their time indoors.

Perhaps this subject is an additional link between the severity and timing of the influenza and other diseases and the strange weather that occurred during the Fatima Apparition.

D. Other Connections to Health and the Apparition

Another interesting timing correlation involving health was the invention of semisynthetic opioids, which occurred around 1917. These drugs are now being taken by millions of people today and the rate of death from these medications is climbing alarmingly. The use of these drugs can lead to addictions, and set a path to illegal drug use, which can result in poverty, birth defects, violence, and a break up of the family.

The leaflet of some of these medications provide cautions concerning prescribing due to individual tolerance for them. This factor is probably dependent on the function of the digestive system's ability to assimilate and cleanse efficiently. If these medications were to accumulate without close monitoring recommended, serious complications including sudden death might arise.

If health care to correct the root cause of pain is not provided, this can result in abuse of medication, especially for veterans, or those who are covered by government plans that are struggling to provide quality and timely services.

Living near three military bases, I have had heart-wrenching encounters with veterans and active military concerning their health, lack of access to medical treatment, and actions to take their own lives when on multiple medications.

Since around the time of the apparition, the study of, and later reliance on, medications for all forms of "diagnosis" and maintenance of health has become the acceptable norm. The long term, wide range impact has not underwent the test of time, although rising health care costs are a large problem in this country.

The continual expansion in side effect warnings on medications, including non-psychiatric medicines, especially for possible suicidal behavior, is a concern. The side effect for taking a medicine for a non–life threatening illness could be death.

While drugs may not be the only reason for suicidal behavior, avoiding anything that can lead to this permanent tragedy should be a priority. Is prayer and peace present when a person makes the decision to kill themselves? What will happen to the soul once the person dies? Was this also related to the 1917 warning concerning the existence of hell?

The image of St. Padre Pio in the photograph, and his model hospital, which was focused on physical, spiritual, and mental health is important to consider, especially for institutions owned by religious organizations that strive to continue to uphold the sanctity of life.

For many reasons, modern medical resources have become increasingly strained. Having worked with health insurance professionals for many years, it became obvious over time that health care costs would become prohibitive since the general principles of risk by insuring "known losses" have been disregarded.

As a Master Herbalist, being aware of the overall impact of poor lifestyle choices and exposure to toxic substances has clearly reflected the potential for declining health, even in young people.

Regulation and corresponding shifts in cost sharing and patient care have pressured health care providers' solvency, opening the door to evolving profit-driven corporate management. This "business" approach to medical care has threatened the basic missionary concepts that led to the creation of charitable health care systems. The old charities were based on Biblical teachings, especially the life and teaching of Jesus Christ, which offered compassion and care for the sick and the poor, as well as miraculous healing through divine intervention.

Profit and affordability have resulted in a temptation for health care providers to make business-based life and death decisions, especially for the poor or the elderly. This is evolving into a trend for "legalized" termination of life including abortions.

When recently reflecting on the acquisition of the photograph and the events that occurred so long ago, questions began to come to mind:

- What if Elizabeth's husband's first doctor offered the newly evolving legally acceptable "death pill" option after he was diagnosed with his terminal condition?

- What if Elizabeth was not proactively helping her husband who could have been on medication that might impact his ability to make the life or death decision?

- What if Elizabeth and her husband did not have access to another physician that was more positive thinking and open minded to all options of treatment?

- Can't miracle healing occur at any time, and how much does that cost?

- What impact does the condoning and assistance of the early cessation of life have on the people involved, including the practitioners?

Could the unexplainable events have been masterfully planned over decades to bring forth the importance of the sanctity of life at this critical juncture, especially for leaders and professionals who have vowed to protect and cause no harm?

There have been several U.S. hospitals in which modern Marian Apparitions have been reported to be witnessed. Perhaps there is a connection?

CHAPTER 4:

SIMPLE SOLUTIONS FOR HEALTH AND ABUNDANCE

A. Inexpensive Natural Solutions

Living in North Carolina, the "Tar Heel State," further prompted my research into the local lure and historical value of natural solutions, especially the evergreen species of trees, for improving indoor air and health. The use of the trees and plants that grow abundantly as a beautiful gift to help people, especially those who are poor, or could not help themselves, became apparent.

As mentioned previously, the book I located from 1914 that cited instances of people being cured of consumption involved the use of kerosene. While this seems rather inappropriate or dangerous, kerosene was at one time used by many medicinally. The book contained convincing testimonial stories. Exactly how the kerosene was processed was not provided in the book.

Many discussions with local elderly, including farmers and their families, brought great insight into lost remedies such as kerosene. Many of the old cures were derived from pine. They were inexpensive, and commonly used successfully to keep people who lived in our remote coastal community healthy without harmful side effects. Many people whose ancestors consistently used pine, including pine turpentine and kerosene, were reported to live productive lives into their nineties.

During a discussion with a pharmacist who owns an old, private, local pharmacy, he lamented about the changes that have occurred in his trade, and said many elderly still come into his store to search for what was simple, natural, popular, and effective.

While reviewing information about old apothecaries for a volunteer position at an old historical settlement, it was fascinating to learn about their work. Many of the old natural formulas addressed basic challenges and were sold by pharmaceutical firms. They included:

- intestinal or blood cleansers that were used to remove parasites or toxins for permanent weight loss/and maintenance of health;

- retorts and distillers for plant oils;

- formulas to increase phosphorus levels to prevent arthritis and other calcifica
  tions;

- homeopathic remedies for a myriad of conditions; and

- natural liniments, disinfectants, and salves.

Unfortunately, many of the old medical practitioners unknowingly used heavy metals such as lead and mercury in their practices. This could have impacted mortality. There was, however, a definite pattern of longevity when the plants were wisely used. For example, *The Apothecary in Colonial Virginia*, written by Harold B. Gill, Jr. included a copy of a record of an apothecary billing a client for curing their cancer. A cure for leprosy was also noted.

During my archive search, I was delighted to discover an old book called *Medicology*. This book was written in 1904, and was designed to be a practical family guide for health. It was a collaborative effort of several very prominent Medical Doctors from London, New York, and Philadelphia. Oddly enough, it discussed the value and practice of using pine derivatives for consumption (TB) and other life threatening illnesses, including appendicitis. It also extensively detailed how important it was for buildings to be designed to avoid moisture build-up and the significance of clean air for maintaining good health. Another "coincidence" since so many of the famous religious figures from long ago had suffered from the respiratory diseases especially TB.

Aside from the two archived books concerning pine, the historical prevalence and value of pine trees for humanity is noteworthy. In 1933 President Franklin D. Roosevelt proposed the Civilian Conservation Corps (CCC) to solve two problems. It helped employ Americans from age 18–26 who were unemployed because of the economy. It also revitalized the forests. So many young people are struggling economically now, what a great way to help them and replenish one our countries' most valuable resources, the pine.

The USEPA has, over time, approved many formulas derived from pine for use as disinfectants in public places including: hospitals, schools, beauty salons, and so on for mold, mildew, virus, bacteria and other pathogens. There are details of pine's effective use to disinfect against pathogens that cause "uncurable" diseases including herpes and very resistant virus and bacteria. Pine oil diluted with water was an old solution for mosquito control and has been studied for its value as a larvicide.

The pine derivatives were obtained from the tree and processed in a variety of ways. Old timers often tapped the pine tree and used the liquid or resins for health. Pine was reported to be used for fuel, printing ink, paint, medicine, moisture control for buildings, and many other purposes. It was basically replaced by petrochemical by-products that were harmful to human health, especially benzene. Over time, benzene seemed to replace the pine. Why? Tapping a pine tree or making tea from pine needles did not bring large profits. Although, historically, North Carolina exported a significant amount of pine derivatives.

Modern benzene was developed by a scientist in the mid-1800s while watching the molecules dancing over a flame. It became popular in the late 1800s, which is coincidentally near the time modern researchers traced mitochondrial damage linked to diseases like cancer, which was becoming a more widespread problem.

Modern studies have been conducted for pine's promising impact on cancer and reversing DNA damage. One can search Pub Med, Pine Oil, and Cancer and locate the studies. Since pine is a natural phenolic compound, it may offset the impact of petroleum-based products that contain harmful solvents that are so prevalent in our modern world. This may include plastics, dyes, drugs, pesticides, biocides, weapons, and fuels. These substances are known for their adverse impact on health, especially cancer.

Evidently, the evergreen species has been studied in Russia for the ability to reverse the side effects of radiation produced by the Chernobyl incident. The Russian government has recently granted land to organizations such as, The Ringing Cedars of Russia, in a concerted effort to increase exportation of domestically produced products and improve the health of the Russian people.

Both frankincense and pine studies have a commonality. The pine and frankincense species of trees (as well as myrrh) all ooze medicinal resins. Frankincense and pine both have a connection with the mysterious "pineal gland," which had the historical name of the "pine cone." The pineal gland has been studied for its impact on contemplative prayer. Old symbols of pine cones have been reported to be seen at the Vatican.

Frankincense and myrrh trees may be threatened with extinction due to the current economic conditions and the escalation of fighting in the parts of the world where the trees are grown. It would be very sad to have these symbolic and useful trees lost forever. This may perhaps be another reason for the unexplainable presence of the changed images in the bottom of the photograph after the Epiphany.

Fortunately, pine that grows so abundantly can also produce positive results to keep the frankincense and myrrh tree resins from being over harvested. Planting frankincense and myrrh trees is a wise investment. It takes many years for the trees to become productive, so it is imperative that protection of these trees occur. Saving the trees is mentioned in Revelation. "Rough-hewn trunks as of a cork tree" was also mentioned as part of the scene in the Third Fatima Secret.

While there maybe countless numbers of reasons for a miraculous event, there have been several instances, including Fatima, where Marian Apparitions occurred near trees, especially the pines species. The Caritas Community located near Birmingham, Alabama, has a very large pine tree called Father Pine. This community of people have reported receiving many messages from The Blessed Virgin Mary, including a visitation by the tree.

B. Assisting Charities, Schools, and the Military to be Healthy and Save Money

Since the photograph was acquired, a recurring solution to help the charities and schools became obvious. The challenges could be addressed through the education and use of inexpensive, naturally available resources that are simple to make.

Traveling to places in the Caribbean and Latin America, I noted that abundant plant matter was available. This plant matter had many uses. The problem was exportation rules and costs. In the United States, the pine seemed to be one of the most abundant resources, although there are others. I began experimenting with ways to procure and use pine without harming the trees' further growth.

One useful pine derivative was obtained through distillation. Pine needles, like other abundant plant resources, can easily be distilled to produce a hydrosol and essential oil. Essential oils are gaining great popularity even in hospitals. The pure pine hydrosol has many uses, including multi-purpose cleaning and for external application when diluted.

Distillers can be purchased relatively inexpensively. A scientific school supplier sells inexpensive distillers for educational purposes or personal use. It is almost as easy as making soup. All that is required is washed plant material, pure water, water for cooling the apparatus, and a heat source. Within a few hours, the distillation results in the production of many liters of hydrosol and a concentrated essential oil.

The use of botanicals, especially distillation, could simply and inexpensively help address serious issues threatening health and prosperity. A model to assist charities could be as follows:

A business or individual donates either $500 or $1,000 to a non-profit such as a school, orphanage, mission, or church group. The donation is used to buy either a 30-gallon or 50-gallon distiller. If the non-profit produced around 220 distillations a year, 660 liters/1,540 liters of hydrosol could be obtained using native plants like pine needles. A very powerful, pure essential oil would also be produced. Larger distillers could also be produced from scrap metal that could distill 100 gallons of hydrosol.

The hydrosol is very concentrated, so if diluted based on three teaspoons of hydrosol to three cups of water, one distillation could produce many, many bottles of multi-purpose cleaners. This formula can be adjusted for strength.

The labor needed to harvest the plant matter, wash it, and distill it would be assumed by volunteers, students, or even a program like Roosevelt's CCC. The military or veterans could produce distillers and distill the pine that grows abundantly around many military bases. This may assist the veterans to be productive and provide help with detoxification for the chemicals to which they are routinely exposed. It would also save money on cleaning products. Pine has chemicals called phenolic compounds. Phenolics, as well as thymol products, (from thyme plants), are approved for use in cleaning by The Department of Education.

Non-profits producing botanical by-products could give back to the donor who would receive a return on their investment by saving money on purchasing cleaning supplies. There is a non-profit called Thistle Farms that supports women who are abused or addicted to drugs by producing natural beauty care products including distillation of lavender.

There is another organization called Greenerways Organic that is marketing essential oils and plant matter produced by farmers in India. The farmers, due to their religion, can receive only a very small yearly income. A portion of the company's profit is returned to their community for improvement of life, building sewer systems, and so on. The essential oil for outdoor pesticide use is certified organic, and is being used on trucks for pesticide control, especially mosquitoes, by government entities in the United States. It smells great and is cost effective and safe for the environment and humans. Why not use it? The company is creating other essential oil products for indoor use.

An important consideration is the impact on health, since pure botanicals are beneficial, rather than harmful (toxic). Synthetic pesticides are generally formulated to impact the neurological system of the insect. Therefore, the impact on humans, especially neurological health, might lead to an increased prevalence of disorders such as attention deficit and autism that have increased significantly in children. In addition, asthma in children is very common and synthetic chemicals may exacerbate this condition. In many pesticide formulas, there is an added chemical that has been studied for its harmful impact on the liver's ability to eliminate toxins. Using Certified Organic products would reduce the toxic load and result in further savings on health care costs and increased productivity.

If projects such as these were duplicated in many areas, millions of bottles of natural botanical products could be produced to support charities with a minimum investment in distillation equipment. The products could also be traded to provide diversity of botanical compounds that have different properties.

This concept can be applied to other plants such as eucalyptus, cinnamon, and lemongrass that grow prolifically in many regions where there is extreme poverty.

Use of the oils could help in places that have been damaged due to hurricanes or other natural disasters without importing expensive chemicals that may be toxic, and that provide financial support for radical groups that cause harm. Supporting the missions, schools, monasteries, and convents is a smart investment. The cycle of poverty could be broken.

In addition to the disinfecting properties of many botanicals, there is also USEPA-approved value for repelling disease-carrying rodents.

The purchase and trade of other natural, non-toxic products, such as candles, incense, soaps, and so on that are crafted by charities and schools has great potential.

C. The Value of Using Natural Alternatives for Cost Reduction and Health

Is it a coincidence that Planned Parenthood came into existence by Eugenics, whose type of work was duplicated during World War II, before the 1917 apparition? Fatima events clearly involve the warning concerning life after death. The first year of life and the last year of life tend to be the most expensive. So, is there a modern, financially motivated incentive to end life before it begins and prematurely when it would naturally end? If so, the solution would require low cost options for maintaining health and life.

There has been a positive resurgence of efforts for organizations to embrace other more natural approaches to health that have been well documented as effective. This includes using alternatives to human cells that may be obtained through the killing of fetuses. Protecting life is one of the main messages from the Fatima Apparition, so it is appropriate to discuss the current state of health care delivery and offer healthy solutions that protect and promote life as part of this book.

As an example, there is an 85-year-old supplement company called Standard Process that many years ago patented the use of specialized animal cell therapies to assist humans to regain health. Animal cell glandular therapy has been approved for use as a pharmaceutical drug for thyroid conditions for many years. Obviously, this approach works.

This company also saved over 50% on benefit costs for their employees by incorporating whole food nutrition, exercise, and non-invasive medical treatments. They have developed an organization called Cultivate for other employers who are interested in saving on employee benefits while improving the lives of their employees and their families.

There is an increased emphasis by many other employers to invest in innovative, more "natural" approaches in their work environments. Increased productivity and the cost of medical care is a driving factor. There are many who realize that going back to basics as created for the maintenance of health, while respecting human ingenuity for assisting with acute, life threatening medical conditions, is the wisest option. Increases in health plan deductibles and other cost sharing will prompt people to continue to search for ways to prevent illness and use more natural approaches to assist non-acute medical conditions.

The current health care system in the United States, especially for family practitioners, often creates incentives for physicians to expedite care. The quick, band aid approach to treating symptoms can lead to inappropriate care. Adverse side effects perpetuate the need for medical intervention and result in spiraling health care costs.

When reviewing health claims during the 1970s and early 1980s, the frequency of claims for diabetes, heart disease, cancer, and other illnesses was notably less. Rarely were claims for mental conditions submitted. This enabled employers and insurers to offer higher benefit levels at lower costs. Claimants were not usually on numerous daily prescriptions. However, this changed when the pharmacy cards became popular, and the structure of many benefit plans was modified to include low co-payments on physicians' office visits and medications. Over time, the attempt to offset expensive inpatient and outpatient hospital treatment by shifting costs to cheaper forms of care drove up medical costs due to heavy reliance on medications for treatment of symptoms rather than on maintaining healthy lifestyles (i.e., "I'll just take a pill").

Inflated and ineffective management of health care can have a significant impact on the ability to compete with employers (competitors), especially those who do not need to offer benefits to retain employees. Many countries also embrace the importance of regulation to protect the health of their citizens from documented hazards in modified food, heavy metals, and so on. In addition, many cultures have embraced their ancestors' traditions of medicine that are relatively inexpensive and pose little risk of harmful side effects.

The United States has reached the point where the young, who should be in optimum health, and the old, who are at increased risk for ill health, are both requiring medical treatment. As a result, there is a greater challenge for health plans to provide coverage, so costs are shifted to individuals. The burden of these increased costs has the potential to negatively impact prosperity and the ability to share and serve others. Those who are unable to care for themselves tend to suffer the most when resources dwindle.

This perpetuates the cycle of poverty. Reducing payment to providers can result in substandard care that, in the end, can increase costs. Not getting to the real root cause of the health care problem is like squeezing a balloon.

The Native American, African American, and apothecary tradition of health care have been replaced in the United States with control of the use of synthetic substances. The old traditions face very tough scrutiny and their effectiveness is often unacknowledged. Some are even persecuted for their efforts to educate and assist people who have chosen a more natural path to health.

For example, there are botanicals that can assist with addictions and replace pain medicine. Addiction to pain medicine is sometimes referred to as an "epidemic." In many parts of the world there are successful clinics that rely on ibogaine, a plant to assist with severe addictions. Cannabidiol (CBD) oil with high tetrahydrocannabinol (THC) content has been studied for its value to help with addiction. Unfortunately, these remedies are illegal in this country. Kratom is an herb that has historical value for both pain and addictions. This herb was going to be outlawed in this country but petitions to maintain the ability to purchase it legally have kept the herb on the market. The government and health care providers should investigate how these plants can be of use in a supervised clinical setting in this country.

The studies and statistics regarding the impact of varying types of stress or negative emotional patterns that contribute to "dis-ease" are noteworthy. The stress from the ability to keep up with health care costs is a vicious cycle that can perpetuate poverty.

Complementary medicine will sometimes correlate a particular type of emotional pattern to symptoms or illnesses. For example, some believe that holding in deep seated hatred can be linked to liver issues and cancer. Fear may be considered to cause heart attacks. If true, the importance of maintaining a positive, trusting, forgiving attitude would be imperative for optimum health.

Why not embrace the concept of promoting life, while increasing abundance using what was created for that purpose? Wasn't that an important part of Jesus' ministry and many well-respected religious figures while on Earth? Didn't God say plants were good right from the beginning of creation? Weren't the leaves to be used as medicine? Perhaps this is another reason for the Fatima photograph changes.

CHAPTER 5:
CLOSING SUMMARY

It is not the intent, nor would it be appropriate, for this book to detail all of the events that occurred during the Fatima 1917 Apparitions. There are books written on this subject based upon eyewitness accounts of what occurred.

While it is impossible to figure out the unlimited implications and ramifications of unexplainable events of religious significance, the series of mysterious occurrences concerning the 1917 Fatima Apparitions as they coincide with what is happening in the world today strongly point to the immediate need to implement change to protect the Earth and life. Also, taking time to contemplate whether life exists after death is important.

The symbolism of the original sin by Adam and Eve, or first people, reflects the human tendency to be unsatisfied with God's presence and that which was created as a gift. Instead, we search after the knowledge of good and evil so we can improve on that which has already been deemed "good." Never before in the history of humankind has life been so severely threatened by our self-centered arrogance and reverence toward technology.

We have the choice to create our own misery, or to be satisfied with love. Although human intelligence is a gift when we are truly well intended and guided by God's love.

Hopefully the other Fatima warnings of what could occur will be avoided through prayer and humankind living in peace.

Perhaps if more people reflected on these messages and important current events, the world could experience great, positive change. Since we all have been given free will, it begins with changing yourself.

Listed below are a series of thoughts and reflections you may wish to ponder as you contemplate the Fatima event, what is happening in the world, and how it has and will affect your own personal life:

History has demonstrated that "inhuman" thinking on a mass scale can result in complacency and acceptance of genocide and massive destruction. Has modern society eroded how you view the value of life in all its forms?

Reflecting on your own acceptance of practices which threaten the sanctity of life is something each one of us should consider. The victim could end up being you or a close loved one.

The new age of technology became increasingly popular after the apparitions. The impact on human conscience relating to behavior that would not otherwise occur is unknown. The use of harmful manmade substances can cause widespread adverse health, which can include the slow seepage of mental health. The potential for losing the ability to think well is something to take seriously.

It is well documented that exercise, clean air and water, whole foods, and stress management do protect health and the ability to think clearly. Why not invest time, resources, and efforts in your personal and work life to safeguard your physical and mental health? If you don't take care of yourself, who will?

If great signs and wonders occurred due to divine intervention, would you be led by the media and the people living in our modern world to dismiss the event as a publicity stunt that occurred as a result of technological advances? What happens to faith when the "miracles" are consistently dismissed as a by-product of human intellect and technological advancement? Ironically, the photograph copies came into existence as a result of technology to take and copy pictures, but they are an example of how we choose to use our gifts. Could photography be an example of one medium of communication chosen to help us witness a miracle without relying on the testimony of others?

Watching and helping yourself be personally aware and open to unexplainable gifts of love, no matter how small, is a good way for you to raise awareness and enjoy true peace. Spending time surrounded by nature and taking time to quietly reflect on love is a way to witness the truths in life.

What will become of the morality of our children if there is no awareness of the severe ramifications of the need to follow the basic rules set down for us to live peaceful, loving lives? Will your soul and the souls of those you love rest eternally in peace if morality is dismissed? If you do not desire to develop a relationship with God, then what will happen when your body dies?

Protecting close relationships and reinforcing the importance of respect will help future generations to desire to protect the value of all life. Taking time to examine your own personal relationship with that which is divine is time well spent. Teaching others about the existence of the divine is a fulfilling investment in your life purpose.

Are you following your unique path to receive the optimum amount of happiness in your life or is your thinking being limited ? Do you know yourself? If you don't, how can you love yourself, follow your own unique path, love others as yourself, and be happy and truly fulfilled? How are you going to receive what you want if you don't know what you truly want or don't ask for it? Who suffers if this is left up to someone else or ignored? Like maintaining good health, "It's a do it yourself operation."

An exercise to identify your own path to happiness can be achieved by following a few simple steps:

- First, write down everything that you personally consider to be fun. Contemplate your unique gifts and talents and what you are honestly and positively passionate about. What puts you in your positive zone of creating, producing, accomplishing, and so on?
- Next, make a list of what you are thankful for; then express your gratitude to God.
- On a daily basis, imagine what would be fun and the best outcome that would make you smile. Write down and ASK your loving Father God for what you would like to have happen in your life. As you go through your day, speak of it happening and let others reaffirm it. According to the Bible, our spoken words are very powerful.
- Believe the best outcome will happen because your God is a God of love. Then give concerns over how and when it will happen to God and follow where you are directed. Listen quietly and observe. Being in an intimate relationship with God is a beautiful gift.
- This is a very good exercise to teach children so that they get to know them selves, pursue the path that brings true fulfillment and joy, while building their relationship with God.
- Won't we all live happily and abundantly sharing and benefiting from each others' ability to offer to the world our unique gifts through God's Grace and supreme generosity?
- Having faith in the existence of an all loving, powerful, divine presence that guides us with Grace is good. What exactly is the down side of loving to love God?

May the information in this book help you to follow your unique and special path to make your life and the world a better place.